THE FLYING DAYS

Coyla Barry

Laureate Series

CAROLINA WREN PRESS
Durham, North Carolina

Editor: Andrea Selch
Design: Lesley Landis Designs

Cover Image: "Sunset Flight" © 2014 Don McCullough

The mission of Carolina Wren Press is to seek out, nurture, and promote literary work by new and underrepresented writers, including women and people of color.

Carolina Wren Press is a 501(c)(3) nonprofit organization supported in part by grants and generous individual donors. In addition we gratefully acknowledge the ongoing support of Carolina Wren Press's activities made possible through gifts to the Durham Arts Council's United Arts Fund.

Library of Congress Cataloguing-in-Publication Data

Barry, Coyla.
[Poems. Selections]
The flying days / Coyla Barry.
    pages cm. -- (Laureate series)
ISBN 978-0-932112-98-9
I. Title.

PS3602.A8376A6 2014
811'.6--dc23

2014006196

ACKNOWLEDGMENTS

My profound gratitude is extended to the Black Socks Poets who have been reading and improving these poems with me for over twenty years. I treasure their skills and friendship.

Carolina Wren editor Andrea Selch has shepherded this book to publication with dedication and sensitivity. It has been my own private creative writing seminar.

Many thanks to the editors of the following publications where some of these poems or previous versions of them appeared.

The Asheville Poetry Review: "That Summer"

Cæsura: "Bluegill" (also published in the *Billee Murray Denny Poems*)

The Greensboro Review: "Watching for the Perseids"

The Independent Weekly (Durham, NC): "Perimeter Problems"

Irene Leache Poetry Prizes: "Chautauqua Summers" (published as "Upstate Summers")

Kakalak: "Blue Heron on the Nest" and "Gratitude"

The Lyricist: "The Last of Him" (published as "Bed of Nails") and "Fishermen"

The New Virginia Review: "Cutting His Hair"

Nimrod: "Failings 1" (published as "Sullen April")

The Pedestal Magazine: "Stargazer"

Pinesong: "Intermittent"

The Sound of Poets Cooking: "Risotto"

Southern Poetry Review: "Rain Crow"

Tar River Poetry: "The Plan," "Squalor" and "Solar Eclipse"

CONTENTS

For Don, Gair, and Peter

And still, the long slanting days pull us in,
the warmth, the pitch of the hills,
and everything in us wants to give over again—
Only a little further,
a hand's extending, a single word;
the mirage, beautiful, beckons us on.

—*JANE HIRSHFIELD*

from
CREATURE
AND CREATURE

FISHERMEN

Beach-walking in November, I watch
        them watching
for a sign, remembering when
        a twenty-pounder

                yanked on a lure out there
and along the beach,
        the hallelujah
brought the men alive.

Everything I see argues the sea's
        emptiness: whitecaps,
winter wind, slatey water.
        But this time,

when their bodies haul and bend
        in a beautiful ecstasy,
the sleek fish plunging
        through the air

into the arms of the believers,
        the prizes coming
like answered prayers,
        I covet,

                just for a moment,
the stance and faith that brings
        such flesh
out of the mouth of the storm.

BLUEGILL

The pond skin tucks here
and there with the delicate *O*
of his lips. He mouths
the pollen film and sultry air

for news of a breeze bearing
humidity and grasshoppers.
Fins fanning, he propels
his small fuselage

backwards to a cave
of cattails scouting
weeds before gliding
off to lip the sky again.

A dragonfly dips down—
merged concentricities
radiate like shared memories
across the pond.

Not all of us here puckered
are in the water. Our mouths,
sweat-sweet and powdery
with hay-bloom,

taste of everything
a warm fall day can distill
into a moment's
postponement of winter.

In a poised cast of lines
singing out from reel and grommet,
we're caught in the pond rim's
reflection and flung up and up

into the blue expanse overhead.
Then a tail-swish
and down-tug of bobber,
and a frail sliver, a spill

of green and gold,
twitches and jerks
onto the dock. Thrown back
into his element,

he leaves a touch
of bluegill on our fingers,
fresh as life itself,
like amnion, the first pond.

AT THE ROOKERY

Two hours I've watched the riotous ardor
of great egrets crowding the island
across the water. The air is edgy with their squawks.

When a male cautiously approaches, flapping down
beside a chosen female's adjusting body,
she gives some gesture of acceptance

I can't discern, and he mounts with splayed feet
the white expanse of her back. The jostlings
and cries make evolution real and now.

Meantime, it seems, every tree holds
in its upraised branches a nest or two,
where patient females, like plumed hats

in a window display, huddle on messy bowls
of twigs. The snout and eyes of an alligator
hardly ripple the water as it slides by the shore,

and I shiver for any runty fledgling that might fall.
Above me, on the wooden tower, two women
in biking spandex have laid their helmets aside,

and are kissing tenderly, oblivious.
The heat and throb of this South Carolina wetland
rushes into me, and I am egret, biker,

every creature's body graced by spring
and ready for another of its kind,
lovers all, nerves and veins squawking.

RAIN CROW

Just now at noon I heard him,
keow-keowing deep in the leaves,
pin feathers pricking,
hollow bones beginning to hum.
Air changes before a storm,
gathers texture and weight,
settles in scalp and skull
like fine grit. When he calls,
I move to the window to scan
the highway, the liquid mirages
shifting over the roadbed, conservative
leaves unfurling like fronds of coral
at the turn of the tide. Breathing
open-mouthed, parched for something
I can never name or pray for,
I watch woods becoming green caves
I loved and feared as a child,
full of rustle, visions. Thunder,
just out of hearing, stokes
the stillness and even the sparrows subside
in the hedgerow as the first drops
fall. A gleam from behind a cloud
picks out a glossy profile, reticent
in the sycamore, its mocking eye
the center of a maze, glimpsed and lost
as he slips into shadow, the way
of the cuckoo and the far-fetched world.

CROWS, AGAIN

They come at any hour of the day, a gang
of them, patrolling the treetops, calling to each other.
She hears their cawing in the mid-morning silence
as they swoop at a neighborhood owl,

perched at his favorite hole.
When they fly at him with hoarse cries
and jabs, the owl stands fast. The pine branches
quiver with hopping and thrusting.

She knows memories can devil like crows,
the way they show up, flocking in
from the edges of consciousness
with disheartening regularity:

first husband, baby on her lap,
his voice bearing down, vibrant
with arrogance—a mean crow
that never fails to draw a little blood.

The blind date crow with lewd hands
and mouth, that flaps around her head
when she drops her guard or the pawn dealer's
tin snips biting off her diamond.

And more often these days, the face
of her mother, anemic and wasted,
rises from oblivion even at parties
and she has to keep talking to stay composed.

Why can't she be like the owl
and ignore these tormentors—remember her father
at the podium, instead of the death's head
bone-bright where he used to be?

Sweet moments would be such consolation.
Despite her best efforts, they slip away
into vagueness. It's the tricksters
that return, relentless and bullying.

The crows get bored, move off as carelessly
as they arrived. Ruffling his body, the owl blinks
and blinks again. Shrugs out his wings,
and floats soundlessly into the woods.

SUDDEN SQUALL
for Grey

It's the drool and fury
of a baby before feeding, a torrent
of anticipation shattering
the dream-wrapped, pre-dawn hours,
a sleet of guilt raking the heart
as it fights off arousal.

It's a thunderclap of need,
ear-splitting, gut-rattling,
capable of bringing
a household to its knees,
the crack of hunger
implacable as lightning.

Like a mouth at the breast,
all's peaceful after its passage.
Satisfaction
blankets the landscape,
and, in the distance,
a few hiccups rumble—
fading reminders, early warnings.

SUMMER ANTELOPE

They bolt at the slightest provocation:
                    shadows, gophers, anything motorized.
                    As a matter of principle,
they sprint first, ask questions later

and let me know I'm skittish too—
                    on the alert for put-downs
                    and faint praise, the "don't you think"
enough to send me wheeling and lunging

through barbed wire. I'm always crouched
                    when I'm grappling
                    with words, ready to flee
when the guard animal gives a snort.

Ten years they've mostly avoided our spread
                    on their summer wandering—
                    small herds and lone males
grazing the short-grass expanse of prairie

beyond our border, hiding away
                    in shallow gullies and far-off sage-brush,
                    counting on eyesight
and speed to outwit predators.

This summer they found our alfalfa
                    and made it home base—
                    groups drifting in like so many
village folk at the town well,

most of the does coming to rest in the hay,
                    tan against green,
                    a few kids wandering,
the stern black-horned buck on patrol.

Today the drone of noonday flies in August haze,

links us, creature and creature,
instincts lulled,
me here scribbling, antelope browsing
nearer than ever, the shared ease
letting the words fly,
while the sentinel there
keeps an eye peeled for the both of us.

from
SWIMMING WOMAN
POEMS FROM MONTANA

SLEEPING OUT

A branch cracks and I'm yanked
in memory to one of our first nights
here when the earth gave a shiver,
and behind our shallow mouthfuls
of air, we heard something massive
coming through the high grass.
A long pause and then an odor,
rank and oily as old tallow,
reached us bedded in our tent.
Bear, I heard you whisper, and felt
your body ease toward the flap.

The stars were out but the bear,
or its fetid avatar, had melted
into the dark. Unsleeping,
we lay in our bedrolls,
still almost not breathing,
tasting the air for a trace
of that animal stink. A thrill
of fear, at last, began to nudge
our stuttering hearts
into a slow, but louder, clamor.
You rolled against me then
and we turned aroused flesh
to each other, suddenly fervent
in the sway and quiver of nerves.

We're gray heads on clean sheets
now, the tent long gone to shreds
in a hail storm, but our cabin
window stays open on warm nights.
Sometimes a hoof stomps
the ground, a buck snorts
or fur scrapes bark nearby,
hauling us back to the woods
and that strange smell and hot snuffle
that set tame bodies ticking.

CALL AND RESPONSE

The veery's song is a shape in the dusk,
over and over, a spiraling down,
four repeats, calling everywhere
and nowhere specific, but close by,
a body-but-nobody presence making
the wilderness less a solitude.
Watchful beside the beaver pond,
I catch a glimpse, brown, furtive,
an eye-blink whisking into a bush.

The dragonfly poises on a twig.
A strew of leaves rides the swell
of green water behind the dam.
Gnats in a cloud hang over the reeds.
The denizens of the twilight woods
have gone silent. I imagine them
still as stone and on alert.
When I became a sometime Westerner
I went among the wary natives,
making my own small whirl or two,
a migrant missing my cues, with my
"Save the Wolves" bumper sticker
and a preference for beans over beef.

"Very elusive" reads the bird guide—
and I'm ready to give up, when the veery,
loud with claim, sends out another spiral
in the almost-dark, the song-wreath
floating on the air, circling the pond
and me standing at its edge.
Another veery sends back an answer
and what the exchange signals sets me
in an orbit of acceptance,
the shape of a new place letting me in.

DOE AND FAWN

Two sets of clear prints in the mud,
a doe with a fawn out for a stroll
after last night's storm. The fawn's track
weaves left and right across the doe's
straight one until they disappear
together into the weeds.
As you raise your head,
you see them there
behind the barn, the little bully
tugging its slender mother's teat,
her head tipped up, savoring the early
morning sun. Your breasts pull taut
at the memory of swollen flesh pummeled
by baby fists and of nipples yanked
by impatient lips, of sore winter days
when you fell into the old couch,
opened your sopping blouse, and welcomed
your own hungry firstborn to his feed.

TURNING

Sometimes the combination (flies, heat, dust)
turns her crazy and his riding off every day

starts to scrape the heart. She wants
to pick a fight, flaunt that shoulder chip

in someone's face, but she thinks instead
of a long stomp; she leaves at noon.

Nothing like the sun bearing down to aggravate
a burn. She stares at the thickets

of bull thistle and burdock along the trail.
The ditch is silted up to a sludgy trickle,

and a huddle of crows picks at a dead gopher.
The high grass makes her itch. Was it too much

to ask? A day in town and his full attention?
She mutters out her monologue to the brush

closing in as the track rises from the flat.
It's a hard climb and she has no breath left.

At the top of the hill a meadowlark warbles
abundance from a fence post.

Gold breast, black bib, open beak pouring out
the fervor of summer: take a look, drink it up.

Waves on waves of pasture, green to the horizon.
The song gushes in, and it returns her.

NEWLY MINTED

The smell of it—cool, damp, an exhalation
of shade and shallows—hints at violence
as it rises when the plants are bruised,
how the scent clings to bare legs
and wraps sweaty shoulders
in a wreath of urgency.

It's a wildness no bottled stuff can equal,
an ooze of crushed leaves and stab
of green itch when low ground
sucks and pulls. Tramplers
find themselves pricked
into discovery, and roused
to rub and wonder.

Mint spreads in a blue fire, a single shoot
becoming a patch, becoming an acre.
Turns a stream bank into a pallet,
becomes a blanket of coins dropped
by the moon, a silver-edged
invitation to take a handful home
and spend it on a lover.

THE FLYING DAYS

PERIMETER PROBLEMS

Every morning I mist the begonia
but the aphids are winning.

The phone cord is frayed
and must be jiggled for a connection.

And who can sleep with new faces
on the ceiling?

Sometimes I take comfort
in the greed

of waxwings in the holly
and the progress of clothesline kudzu.

Someone talks to me
through the heating ducts.

We discuss the meaning of life
and the good friend

we have in each other.
We know all the old songs.

The mail remains
unread for weeks.

My children say
I'm out of touch.

Far out, I say, and
still circling.

THE FLYING DAYS

A dozen vultures
roosted every evening on the arms
of the high voltage power pole
that rose from our backyard woods.
I watched them through the window
returning like members of a club
settling in for conversation.
When the neighbors' banging of pans
drove them off, I missed them.

When I was young, time was endless—
lazy summer days reading Dickens in the glider,
classes in statistics where the clock hardly moved,
pregnancies that marched at their own glacial pace.
Overnight, in middle age, routine made the days
like vultures, lifting off every morning
to their greasy feasts, back again at dusk.

No one believes the days will end.
That solid flesh will dissolve—and disappear—
until one day monitors
are beeping and the patient wakes up
and finds the days
sitting on the rails of the bed,
wings folded like black umbrellas.
Old friends from the pole,
looking for carrion
and they are not picky.

When I look up now
and find them circling overhead—
sharp eyes, bald red heads,
and canted wings cruising the thermals—
they crane their scrawny necks
and lift my heart.
They are my familiars,
promising another blessed day.

ONE DEEP BREATH
TO THE BARREL FLOAT

Four hours of meanders through
small towns, traffic enough
to drive us mad with impatience
for that cool blue V in the notch
of green hills, for the first dash
off the dock, the launch into summer

and months of freedom for children
and mother away from the city.
Piling out at the gate was like opening
a gift from an uncle in disrepute,
mysterious, dangerous: our personal
playground, the run of the place.

Our swimsuits hung lank on hooks
in airless closets, tangy with mildew.
Clothes flung, shoes shed, I raced
downhill through a lane of tamaracks
to cannonball into the water.

A shining path above, seaweed,
lily vines below, a swish off the boards
and one deep breath to the barrel float.
Boys with oiled tans turned bleached heads
to scan through slitted eyelids
my curves and winter flowering.

Fourteen, fifteen—I keep those summers
polished like silver: every road trip
a re-run of that hot slow car leading
to a cold plunge, every blushing dream
a brazen boy eyeing my cleavage,
and every vacation a jewel box of secrets.

OUTINGS

...*even our failing senses insist on outings.*
—*Carlo Betocchi*

Wizened peppers, for instance—those bombs
in the beans and rice—or a slug of single malt
taken straight. Like the ping in gums
and tongue when lemon slices start to spurt.

Another trip: a glass of good red wine,
one earthy mouthful does the trick.
Even with taste buds on the wane, I'm
off to bliss in every pore and crack.

And here at Trader Joe's, flaming hair,
almost blind, a shopper leads with her nose.
At the flower stall she leans to where
she plunges her face to get a jolt of rose,

and gives my eye a jolt of its own—
a few hundred volts and off I fly.

CRABBING

Tannic water, murky and brown,
and midsummer weed swirling in strands
off the pilings brings sliders to the sun-warmed
bank of the tidal creek.

On a day like this,
a chicken neck dangling on a string
is all that's needed to lure some Blue Claws
for a dinner feast.

Hang a bait,
feel a twitch—then slow hand over hand—
lift the net from below and a fat Jimmy
finds itself in a bucket.

As the dark water
moves by with the tug of the tide,
a half-dozen keepers share its fate
before an enormous snapping turtle

heaves up from the depths
and latches on, not to be dislodged.
Its jaws crack bones to splinters,
rip away half the neck.

Blue-as-sky armor,
spikes at the edges with eyes on stalks
that rise and glare at any threat, the crabs
in the bucket grasp each other's pinchers
in their own ferocious snappers.

Frantic for release
to open water and the creek's fresh turn,
the crab clot seethes, bubbling for oxygen,
and scrabbles a fierce chorus
of drum whisks

against the bucket's metal sides. We pitch
the remaining bait to fatten future dinners
and haul our prizes home

              to set the pot to boil—
the cluster's futile protest like that of foes
who do not yield an inch and end up
losing everything.

DADDY LEAVING

Whenever I arrived
he settled in his chair and launched a tale.
He loved the limelight,
and had some exploit teed up every time
to keep Mom and me
          laughing.

He was famous on two coasts
for the wink and grin
          at the punch line.
He held a party
          riveted:
"The camp-out when the rattler spent the night,"
or "George and I in jail in Fresno…"
No matter I'd heard them all
          a hundred times.

Then I began to notice
          that only Mom and I were talking,
his face turning, from hers to mine,
back and forth,
          eyes trying to track,
          but out of sync.

He had silted up like a pool
          after many rains,
leaving himself behind,

          heading out
to his old boat and the flats off the Keys
to cast for bonefish
          with his cronies,
his small smile and horizon gaze saying

it's warm here and the beer is cold
and the boys and I
          don't talk much.

THE KINGFISHER

coils his toes around a snag,
directs his eyes where minnows slide
and shift like run-on rumors.

Over the pond, a cloud of midges
veils the view. He arrows off
to find another branch and waits.

The sultry afternoon lays
down a sheet of glass, clearing
the water to the bottom.

Bird and creek
become a single thought
stuck at a synapse,

where he poses static
as a stone against
the sky and waits

again until he strikes,
splinters silver,
beaks up a minny,

a flash of greyish blue,
leaving an image
there, and not.

METEOR

From the top of the sky it streaked
white and whirling, turning dark to day
as though the sun itself
had burst through the dome.
We were forking up spaghetti
around a late-night campfire
when the bolt arced over us.
Mouths gaping, we looked
at each other, wide-eyed,
tongues helpless in our mouths.
Night birds, fire pit,
even the creek had fallen mute.

If we were a desperate tribe
assembled in a prayer circle,
passing a cup of shaman's brew
hand to hand to end a drought
or turn back a wind-driven fire,
we'd know the clap of light came
from the fist of an invisible One-of-Many,
a spirit watching us in every tree
and star. Even now these stones
seem to glare and coil their sinews
with hot intent to hurl another
doomsday scrawl across the sky.

BLUE HERON ON THE NEST

Today I stand in the shadow, binoculars
misting over, while the mother heron flies
away to fish, returns to plunge her beak down
one gaping craw after another and takes
to the air again without a minute's rest.
The young ones bob and flap, teeter
and squawk. It's a long way down.

When I hitched a baby on my hip,
spooned oatmeal at a toddler, and handed
round honeyed words with peanut butter,
every day was droplets on a hot plate,
caring and cooking and imminent disaster,
a whirl of diligence every mother knows.

The heron shares her catch and seems to sag
before lifting off over the nest rim.
My own mother tugs at me
from a great distance. Her yellow eye
meets mine as she stalks out of the shallows.

WEANING

The breast does not know
the time has come.

Milk lets down like pollen
in an August cornfield.

The babe is a blooming tassel,
a seed after a rain.

His hands roam under her blouse
like a besotted lover,

a bond unimaginable
before these dizzying trysts.

His hunger cry down the hall—
she hears its summons now

as the brass-bright trumpet
of the future.

When he begins to test the center
of his universe with a sharp new tooth,

he finds himself dislodged to the cup,
a rocky hinterland

where both mother and child, bonds broken,
will mourn through the winter ahead.

THRASHER

Beady-eyed thug, he hustled duff
and thicket, scratching up

a living with a beaky bayonet
other creatures flee from.

Adept at scarfing suet, he twirled
head down on the feeder

while the fat stuff flew
and, true to his name,

he never failed to rout the crowd
with dart and thrust.

In spring he who skulked turned operatic,
perching topmost on a tree

to trill a wheedling repertoire
until his lady jerked his sleeve—

Shut up, you fool—
and led him off to deepest bramble

where in weeks she popped four eggs.
He's busy in her service now:

flying back and forth with bits,
single-minded, meek and dovish.

THE MODEL

Six years old, I am to be
a sculptured head,
sitting on a high stool
in the garage my mother
calls her studio.
She digs in a bucket
for wet clay and thumbs it
against a wire framework.

Sit still, she murmurs,
immersed in her work.
My noses itches,
but I'm determined not to crack.
I watch the clock and never move
a muscle. Not even my eyes roll
when she takes
those enormous calipers
that look like scissors
and measures the width
of my small uptilted skull.

In fading light
she smooths the day's
work. I can hardly
keep my eyes open.
Avid for her gaze,
I drift across the gap
between us, becoming
the head (her doll, I think),
imagining those deft thumbs
against the bridge
of my nose, the slow blade
of her palm at the baby
curve of my lower lip.

Finally she swaddles
the head in dampened rags,
gives the remaining clay
a squirt and seals the bucket.
Dizzy with effort,
I follow her to the house.
At the kitchen counter,
I'm still lifting my chin,
holding my head erect,
not moving, my one art.
Finally, her hand,
closes my eyelids,
the touch I've waited for.

Now the cherub smiles
from its pedestal—
a perfect likeness
she used to say,
the plump cheeks
her little finger
dimpled so carefully
still casting,
all these years later,
for a smile back.

HOMESTEAD LILAC

Its few branches
poke up through the slumped porch overhang:
    the supports buckled,
    the residents gone,
the lilac clinging on despite the roof's demise.

The wife must have planted it
by the steps to bloom where its profusion
    would greet her
    at the open door.
Planting is always a down payment.

For ten years
the gnarly thing has been aging out:
    flowering reduced
    as it struggles for light
in a rubble of shingles and bricks,

but still a pleasure
when I come up the track to admire
    and rest in its shade,
    grateful for the long-ago
impulse of a homesteader making a home.

The house itself,
battered by wind and snow, leans to one side.
    Not a visitor
    or salesman
knocked those long bleak winters.

Today I sit in the sun
where she once stood to look for buds
    and new leaves,
    and, like me,
bask in the rollicking society of wrens.

PRAIRIE SMOKE

The rock-hard ground of the plains
begins to give, leaks a breath of green,
patchy carpets of lavender and pink spread
to the horizon, a sudden swig of wine
for the eye, one of the earliest
and toughest of spring insurgents.

After a few days, the modest flowers droop
and soon give way to seeds—each one
hairy with strands more fragile
and fine than any dandelion ball.
Overnight the carpet has become veil,

rippling silver and gray over the ground.
Up close, each knot of filaments shivers
with expectation and, as the breeze rises,
so do the seeds, a bright cloud
of headlines, nature once again flinging
across the land the news of spring on the way.

SQUALOR

"You've never seen *real squalor*" my mother
used to say, so I was thrilled when "Dingy Doris"
asked me to her downtown apartment overnight.
Her reputation for dubious hygiene suggested
an opportunity. I loved the rickety elevator
and the mute metal door which admitted
three of us—wide-eyed eighth-graders—
into a fringe-draped living room
with a ravaged sofa and shawled chairs.
Behind a beaded curtain amid a welter
of pots, like a witch straight from Grimm,
her turbaned mother uttered an unrecognizable
greeting from a miasma of garlic fumes,
a cigarette dangling from her lips.
In Doris's bedroom: black walls, cobwebby
ceiling, posters of Tarot cards,
and plates of leftover food bedecked
every surface. My eyes roamed swiftly
to verify what my mind could hardly encompass.
The nearest awfulness was positively antique,
the pelt a half-inch thick, the presence
of maggots not unimaginable.
We settled around a low table
and Doris produced two packs of cards
and a bottle filled with fluid
the color of urine. "Vodka and Squirt,"
she whispered. We sipped,
played bridge, and spread an orangey
smear of Velveeta on crackers
until midnight sent us to the kitchen
for sturdier fare, but the fridge was empty.
Doris rang for Chinese takeout (my first):
chopsticks and Moo Shu Pork,
shared with several cats, until we bedded
down together on a pile of Doris's underwear
with a handful of French postcards—
each of which I can still conjure,
my loins tightening and ears turning red.

LOST BOAT

In the marsh's gut,
the ruin of an old coaster leans
                    to starboard,
up to the gunnels in mud, one side stove in,
paint scoured off
            by years of wind-driven sand.

The marsh gasps at low water,
                    sun baking seaweed
to a mat of rot.
            A few fiddler crabs inch
from stands of salt grass
                    to pick
the eye sockets
            of a fish head.

Gulls circle in the noon blaze,
                    flap down
on stranded scallops agape where
            parched hinges
have lost their grip.
                    Soft bodies tick and bubble
            their thirst.

Storm-tight nets knotted
                    a century ago
by callused hands, have frayed
                    to flock and lint.

Under the bulkhead
                    an eight-inch glass float
rolls,
                    planet-blue as earth from space,
            released by rising water,
salvage

from the forgotten boat
        and its captain,
     a ghost in a yellow slicker
       riding the wind
           and paying out his nets
in the teeming shoals of a crystal ball.

THE LAST OF HIM

It's September again,
the month my father locked
his broken pitted teeth
and promised himself
not another
mouthful.

Awake now
these first cool nights
when sleep should
come easily,
I see him in the dark—
jaws agape, head shrunken
and yellow on the pillow,

veined lids
stiffening over the last
of him emptying
from the eyeholes.

Despite our efforts
to slip just one more
morsel of food
or sip of water
into him, he left
on his own schedule.

His old self, sharp dresser,
ad man with prizes,
the daddy who filled my shelves
with books faded long ago.

What comes back
is that face, those stretched lips.
He could be laughing.

STARGAZER

Evening and she has been sitting here
while the sky fills with stars,
an expanse blue-violet and marked
with patterns familiar
      as a nursery rhyme.

Summer nights the hours turn on a slack rope,
and the slow motion of the Archer
and the Swan
      swings her

like the hammock where she first learned
their names from a soft-voiced young man
in a summer yard
      full of honeysuckle.

(Gone to other hammocks
      before Orion crested the horizon.)

And when the picture tatters
into the sudden whirl—debris, dust, fire—
galaxies become when the illusion fractures,
telling her she is
      nowhere and nothing,

she knows not to wait
for the moon to lift its white sail
      above the pines—remembering
      lonely days
when she found the heavens' beauty
      hurtful.

Skin cool now, bare feet on wet planks,
she shivers into her robe,
and steps inside,
        her eye orbiting
the universe of the immediate:

a candle by the bedside,
a wine glass ready for another dollop
        and infinities condensed

to fireflies at the window and cinders
        in the grate.

THE PLAN
for my mother

Seed catalogs were her obsession
that last year, thumbed ragged,
heaped in the bed like blankets,
as if she hoped the muscle-bound
vegetables and flowers, hulking
in their touched-up brilliance,
might seep a healing elixir
into her bones. At the window,
where the cloud of her labored breath
formed and faded on the glass,
her drained face and glazed eyes
mirrored the ruin of the winter yard.
We never knew what to say,
what with her mind wandering
when she talked about hyacinths
and tulips, the show of reds and purples
she predicted come April.
In October an actual pick-up arrived—
Maggiore and Sons—
bearing shovels and mattocks.
Long conferences in the bedroom,
the gardener nodding, her frail voice
murmuring from the depths of the pillow.
Now it's Easter and we stand elbow
to elbow with cousins and companions
we haven't seen in years, grouped
around the birdbath, admiring the beds
in flower just as she devised.
We smile at each other over the daffodils,
catching the drift of their perfume.
She knew where she would be.

SLIPPAGE

It happens so often when you write or type—
letters scrambled, dropped or added,
the aging brain hiccupping like a computer
with a wry sense of humor, making
"dog" into "god," "smile" into "slime,"
and tacking an extra zero on your bank balance.
Or the word itself escapes
like a small brown bird slipping
into the underbrush as you stumble
after it, struggling to name
that once-familiar twitter. I spend
half my conversations skull-rummaging,
"you know" and "the thing you stir with,"
and "Mister Furnace Guy" my lame rejoinders.
It seems unfair that a trusty instrument
should lose its edge and fail you
after a lifetime of flash and steel.
I picture it snoozing away in there,
powered down or out of the country
when the commanding officer rings up.
Squint-eyed at the screen or tongue-tied
at a party, fishing for a phrase that refuses to come,
I'm side-blinded when "perseveration"
pops from my lips, preening its tail
and giving me the old razoo.

SPRING PEEPERS

The warm front
arrives with fanfare.
Piping erupts in the ditches,
swells the twilight
with crescendos of sound.
Seditious, these invaders,
appearing in the bottom of the yard
after last week's rain,
throats at full stretch,
pitching spring
and its urgent clamor.

We sit together
in the open doorway
letting the incursions float
into the crannies
of our winter-worn house.
Green balloons
of *glance and touch*
hover above us
as we sip our wine.
You reach with sly intent
and pull one in.

"PASTURE IN THE MAKING"
[land-for-sale advertisement in the Village Advocate]

In a green confidence
we called from the city,
picturing trim fences,
grassy fields
dotted with ponds
and white-faced Herefords.
Stumps and stubble,
red-dirt plow scars,
and eruptions of boulders
gave the lie.

Half a year later,
rain's washed up arrowheads
and we've learned
the decorum of weeds.
Brambles gaining
a foothold look like
they'll be blackberries
come August. Today
they're full of warblers,
various and wild.

THAT SUMMER

All that summer her husband's eyes
were on any place but home. At night he left
without a word, imagining she didn't hear
as he moved through the toy-strewn living room
like a soldier on maneuvers, until he gained
the hook on the screen door, and rolled
the car on a downhill grade.

Open windows, a tick-tock whippoorwill,
the milk smell of chenille when she went
to nurse the baby, and then to stand
at the first-born's head, reciting to herself,
while the children slept, the "what-to-do"
chant she'd crooned for years.

She worked a garden that summer, every day
building sweat in her tanned cleavage, ground-in
earth on her palms. When her husband missed meals
and didn't call, she scraped the roast into the trash
and roamed the leafy rows, the taste of new peas
or radish in her mouth somehow greening her resolve.

But his body beside her was that summer, too.
He came home after midnight to the moon-whitened bed,
and found her glossy and lotioned from the bath,
no nightgown, the sheet turned back.
Mute necessity drew flesh to flesh.

Corn grew to ripeness, squashes swelled.
Tomatoes on the sill plumped to readiness
and sweetened. Sometimes she heard rain
on the leaves, moisture flooding tap roots,
a breeze in the window cool on her skin.
With harvest came her decision at last to leave.

DROUGHT

Today I walk the path, replaying
last night's snip and bicker. A heron makes
its slow way step by step, picking at dried snails.

Like an unblinking eye, the sun's disk
starts to show through the clouds. At pond's edge,
an open sundew shines its pearls in mottled shade.

Bird, plant, sun, all things to gladden,
but still the word-by-word hash and rehash, a blame
war. *You. And you.* The words flew out like wasps

from the weeds, strident zings of ill will.
Restraint can lead to lies, small white fish seen dimly,
circling just beneath the surface.

Months of drought have drawn down
the water, turning ponds to mud flats. The shrunken
pool bubbles up swamp gas. Green algae foams with it.

Love is why lies come, just like your no
when I asked if you once loved more deeply.
The noisy pond goes quiet, not a stem moves,

or leaf. Sundews have closed their fronds.
They, at least, keep their secrets. Some new rain will
reset the balance, giving us room to breathe.

Time will bring us full ponds, and ghostly fish
slipping to cool depths. For now, it's the heron and me,
still picking snails from the muck.

THE HERRING GULL

does not eat a lot of herring
but is very fond of clams, which
usually it swipes from another gull,
screaming riot as it goes.

If a meal is loose and rolling
in the surf, it swoops, plucks,
flies straight up directly to drop the clam
on the parking lot, a perfect strategy
for breaking out the meat.

On this blazing morning the bully
is eyeing my peanut butter. And here
comes a homeless lady, in wool hat
and winter coat, shuffling along to the bins,
So meek and silent, she'll go hungry.

I've seen some gullish humans in my day,
in the bedroom and at the gambling table.
When love's the game, they brag and bark
until they win, then fly to grab another.
Just as I move to share my lunch with her,
the gull shoots in and nicks off my sandwich.

THE SHORELINE ROLLER BARN

loomed in the dark like a birthday cake
bright with a thousand candles,
a beacon visible for miles.

Mary Lou had a driver's license
and her daddy's white convertible,
top down, red leather seats, big fins.

The summer I turned sixteen,
I piled in with her every Saturday night,
the car our ticket to a full tank of freedom

and almost legal beer. The music
jangled like the carousels of childhood,
and soon we were pumping the straightaways

like conquering Amazons, or trolling
for partners willing to steer, as we skated
backwards or swooped side to side.

At intermission we flocked
on our toe wheels to the keg, and a crowd
of eager local boys

with sun-bleached flattops, all of us
throbbing, our limbs on fire and shining
with summertime sweat.

Back on the boards, I flew
and swerved till my toes were raw,
careening like a pin ball off bumpers

until we wobbled for the exits.
Mary Lou got us home at sober speed,
both of us lucky I wasn't driving.

I was lit like a sparkler, and ready to chase
them forever, nights at the Shoreline,
reckless and full of collisions.

GRAMMA

Gramma didn't match the gene pool.
Hugger and screamer in a family
that admonished in hushed tones,
she cackled my name in a crowd
at full-throttle volume,

and set my heart thumping
when she grabbed me up for a kiss,
magenta lips smearing my cheek,
then hauled me to a corner to relate
her latest adventure
("Don't tell your mother.")

Her visits were occasions
for crush and mash, body contact
and a gravelly whisper:
"Have you heard
the one about the aspirin
between the knees?"

Later I learned she covered
her woes with comedy and high drama,
the family always on alert
for the next overdrawn account,
midnight phone call or speeding ticket.

My face bloomed crimson
all over again as she made her exits:
a nip at my ear,
Bristol Cream on her breath,
and her ungirded bosom pressed
against my face.

THE CEDAR
for my grandmother

No plastic flowers in an urn,
just a block of granite with her name

anchors a ten-foot plot all to herself.
On the left, graves from an earlier century
tilt into thickets.

Wild turkeys stalk ahead of me,
slipping through wrought iron
where once she dropped

my hand to point at a doe vaulting the fence.

She who loved flounces and décolletage,
went into the ground in navy gabardine,
never her style.

On the right, polished monuments stand
in ranks downslope from a patriarch.

She wouldn't have wanted
that inferior position, but her lapses and losses
made her an outcast.

Huddling in my raincoat,
pleased but ashamed to have found her
after forty years of neglect,

I notice on a knoll behind the grave,
a ramrod cedar upright
as a lighthouse on a rocky island,

fog-bound in all weathers,
becoming shabbier every year
its beacon moth-balled and its gleam,

like hers, almost extinguished.

SOLAR ECLIPSE
Maine, 1963

Deck chairs and blankets spread to face the sun
in a hill pasture, we new skygazers
rigged our gear and synchronized our watches,

sending silent prayers to Mt. Olympus, to ensure
a cloudless view of what we've traveled far to see,
bearing smoky glass, and cooler-coddled beer.

Restless mothers, stripped down to halters,
lolled beside the babies, painted up in white zinc
like savages, while fathers sipped and placed

their bets on chances for reward when the shadow
made its move. Oiled shoulders and bare midriffs,
quick sidelong glances, spread invitation among us

until the moon's disk, as it bit the sun's,
put on a spectacle that fixed us to the sight—
the shadow's encroaching menace turning

the sun black except for a rim alive with flames,
the image flaring bright inside us even then.
We who played loose on that hill,

babies grown, children now parents themselves,
keep the memento tattooed on some dark brain fold.
To see us no one would believe it,

the fiery ring a mark burned there
by jealous Apollo, watching from the zenith
while we played below. Diana, Goddess of the Moon,

deserved the blame—midday darkness, bird song silenced—
but once avenged, and light began returning,
he claimed his chariot again and rolled it on its way.

CALIFORNIA LEMON TREE

Mornings an oriole grubbed in its branches
for cabbage moths.

Evenings we squeezed pitchers of sours
and stirred up custards

and meringue. I learned his take on Hollandaise
for artichokes.

A tree in every yard out there is weighted
with possibilities,

yellow knobby fruit year round, Palo Alto's gifts
we took for granted.

I've lost touch with him, of course,
old love obscured

the way morning fog flowed in over peaks
to screen the sun.

But lemon sows subversion, plants a seed
in the mind.

This meager wedge sliced now for tea
anoints the air,

calls up sun-stained indiscretions and lemonade
soufflé.

FIREFLY

at my window,
what I wish for
your pyrotechnics
promise. You prick
the dark with code
provocative:
winking shameless
invitation.

Little flasher,
turn your tail on,
make your green
light love light
while I watch and wait.
If only I,
like you, could
incandesce.

BLUE BURIAL

Childhood is only a small blue grave now.
—Mark Doty

A wishbone, a fan, a baby bottle nipple
chewed to the nub, ribbons for the sausage curls
Mother pulled around her finger every morning
were objects I treasured that the left-behind
would place beside mè in my tomb.
If I had died early in an ancient kingdom,

I would have needed the pillow that sent me to sleep
even in foreign rooms where voices raged
in the muffled distance, and no one
came when I called, and the gold piece
Daddy brought me from Fresno,
a pen that used real ink, a diary key.

Also the hardened blood and fur remains
of the baby squirrel I smashed with a flung stone,
a deed I blamed on a younger brother.
And there's a sock I've kept forever
because it smells of pine needles and baby oil
from the last summer I was innocent of sex.

I don't visit my crypt often. It's clotted
with weeds and unmarked by any stone,
but sometimes I have to seek it out,
that midnight, mourning place.
sheltering the totems I've sealed away.
I don't examine them too closely—they whiten
to dust exposed to light and air—but
I need to know they are there with their stories,
secure in the grave, blue as ever.

PLATELET DONOR

My mother's marrow
dwindled to a desert,
after poisons
used to treat her cancer
cured but also killed her.
Her voice faded to a whisper
and her face paled
to gray

between transfusions.
They pinked her up
every time
and she lasted
the months to Christmas.

Now, every few weeks,
the pulsing tubes
lie heavy and warm
against my arm,
my heart beating out
its trusty thump and push.
The platelets, swirled
from the blood,
suspended in plasma,
glow like amber beer
in vinyl bags overhead.

A cookie, a swig of water
and a pat on the back
from the lady with the needle
and I wobble from the lab,
a little pale myself, with a bandage
on the crook of my arm,
cradling a small bruise,
turning purple.

CHAUTAUQUA SUMMERS

1.
Toes-up and drifting
in green weedy water,
on my back divining faces in the clouds—
mother's gray head, daddy's important fedora,
Uncle Mike's mustache puckered
for a smoke ring—

I found a place
beyond the seaweed
where, in the vastness
between fathoms below
and the infinite overhead,
my fantasies grew wings.

2.
The shore lights became a constellation
as the houses began
to settle down and music from the old consoles
flowed across the water.
Anchored in the lily pads with a rod
and a can of bait,
I tried my first cigarette to the strains
of Pachelbel.

Nothing to do but wait,
oars athwart the gunnels,
for the same old perch to tug the line.
Bats swooped circles around the boat,
and a fish dimpled the surface
when it lipped a bug.

When Daddy rang the curfew gong,
I rowed home through the weeds
as slowly as I could, trying to make
the hours last forever,
watching the future—whatever it might be—
bearing down all too soon
out of the dark.

JUNONIA

Sanibel, 1945

First light, low tide,
Daddy and I, heads down,
poked along the wrack line,
turning over flotsam.

He strolled early,
especially at low tide,
this time with me,
sharp-eyed and eager.

No talk, no whining, no stray starfish.
"Ignore everything
but the rare one.
It will jump out at you."

The shell he found that day
sits pride of place on my bookshelf
among the arrowheads and fish fossils,
a perfect three-inch volute,

brown spots on cream background.
He held it a long five minutes
before he handed it over, his warm palm
closing it in my cold fingers.

It was rare, that morning
together, and I still remember it:
his hand, my hand,
imprinted on that shell.

GHOST CRABS

A nickel-sized hole
at the wrack line chucks
a spray of sand.

A pale crab creeps out,
body poised
like a dancer on point.

Up the beach,
more black eyes
in pairs converge

like filings to a magnet,
and the rumor
of claws sweeps across the sand

as a dozen shadows close
on an eel ripped from a hook
by a disgusted fisherman.

Sibilant with effort,
the mound of crabs
thickens and squirms.

The sun gleams
on their several delicate shades
of lavender and straw.

FAILINGS

1.
Five days of rain. Water drips
from a hole in the gutter

when I open a window to test the air.
I breathe for a hint of buds opening,

but the garden floats up a mouthful
of wool and leaf mold.

Alone at the breakfast table, I cup my coffee
with numb fingers, and ponder,

as I often do, my weedy yard and rusty Chevy
while the neighbor's

tidy garden and late-model Beemer prod me
with stabs of guilt.

Then a phoebe lands in the lilac, cocks his head.
His breast, palest yellow,

glows like a torch. He beats there,
a flag, a drum, a summons

to be, be, be. The day turns on
that squeaky hinge,

the flower beds greener, the funky smell
a promise of riches to come.

2.
April pear trees
are bridal in the median.
A skunk's in the compost
and finches crash the feeder,

sort themselves out
in a fuss of jab and peck.
The mulch truck
trails a plume of cedar,

unloads its riches
in my neighbor's driveway.
His back is sore as spit,
he tells me,

leaning on his shovel.
He gives my yard's old leaves
a long look.
Overnight the willows are decked out

in catkins
and pollen drifts in the gutters
like yellow paint.
Anticipation's got big shoulders.

Arrival's a pipsqueak.
When the last spent petals hit the pavement,
already I'll be yearning
for ripe tomatoes.

WATCHING FOR THE PERSEIDS

The first time I saw them
he had led me from the car
to the darkest hayfield
in Ligonier County.
From a north-facing knoll
we scanned the skies:
one, two... ten...
Soundlessly the lights
plumed overhead
until the whippoorwill
announced the moon.

I married the boy
but he's been gone for years and
I spend most evenings indoors
doing what mothers do.
But every August on clear nights
I walk out alone
from a hot kitchen

into the same darkness
where love first found me,
to gaze overhead
and sigh down those long
silver trajectories
to a pasture at haying time,
a girl with all
the time in the world
midsummer, in Ligonier.

SWIMMING TO SLEEP

In the old summer house, the bed
smells musty, like a suitcase of old letters,
the gray sheets threadbare
and damp, the mattress lapsed
in the middle. As I sprawl my body
into its sagging contours, the furnace
belches soot and hungry children
cry to be fed. What I was still haunts
the place in flip-flops and faded denim.
I become her twin, punching at
my childhood pillow, never plump
but flat and flabby now after years
of bedtime whacking. I yawn
and stretch against the foot rail,
pressing spindled comfort into my instep.
My breathing slows, heartbeats
knuckling against my ribs like surf,
and I'm weightless as a wood chip
where everything earlier was turmoil
and demand. Tomorrow's storm is piling up
in the West, its threat a cruel weight,
but tonight I'm a ghost-girl out of school
with tanned shoulders and sun-bleached hair,
pulling arm over arm for the middle of a lake.

SLUMBER PARTY

Now and then I wish I were sixteen again,
sitting on the floor with Lulu and Jane,
drinking ginger ale and whiskey
raided from an absent father's bar,
getting giggly as the glasses empty

and we snuggle together, entwining on pillows,
without the usual "hands off" wariness.
The close quarters have a sultry vibe:
perfume, perspiration, and bourbon
celebrating girl skin heated by contact.

It feels dangerous, that unbidden rush of desire,
bodies relaxing into each other,
the secret examination of shared pleasure,
breast under pink nightie, thigh against thigh.

And soon the record player drops the last
Sinatra and voices hum in unison,
low and almost groaning,
as we drift into dreams of futures

where we wait behind parental warnings,
for arousal and permission,
and the sweet consummations
Frankie's love songs and our eager bodies
have promised us.

SNOW IN CHILDHOOD
Pittsburgh, 1950s

First the silence,
then the silver on the ceiling,
then the leap to the window.
Snow coming down.

Moaning for the pleasure of it,
Sister and I pried open the storm window
and pushed our fingers into six inches of flakes.
Then in scratchy wool and knee-high rubber,
we toured our acre like fat otters,
seeking drifts and mounds to slide down.

Noon cranked up trickles in the gutters
and soot from the steel mills fell
on the new snow's pristine dazzle.
Spirits dropping and frozen to the marrow,
we peeled off sodden leggings, boots full of ice,
and plunged our faces in the wash of steam
from mugs of Mother's horehound tea.

                    Then came the day—
trying to open the window for us,
Mother jammed her hand through the glass,
and an artery began to spurt.
Ten miles from a doctor and 20 inches
building on the ground, she muttered
"pressure points" and "tourniquet"
while I wrapped her bleeding arm
with my bathrobe belt. Addie the maid
roamed the cellar commanding sister
hold the flashlight while she poked
in filthy corners for cobwebs, a remedy
her granny used to bandage wounds.

Leaving me to stanch the flow,
Daddy fled the scene and found a shovel.

After a half an hour feeling helpless,
of reddening towels, and fending off Addie,
I phoned and found a neighbor with a plow.
Mother and Daddy disappeared to the hospital.
Knees trembling, lips quivering, I took to my bed,
sure she was going to die.

Snow followed us, of course, when we moved
to town. Four or five inches sent my father out,
his face resolute, his eyes glittering,
while Mother stood at the window and sighed
at his whirlwind efforts, certain he was courting
a bad back and even cardiac arrest.

We grew in years and free in snow's delights.
Rigged out in ski pants and boots, we escaped
the house to find a neighbor gang of boys
with sleds and snowballs readymade to fire.
Like sparrows we flocked together,
the better to be irresistible targets.

To impress a certain boy, I took his dare
and, jumping off the garage into a drift,
landed hard on the stone pile underneath
and broke my collarbone. Expecting a scolding
at the hospital, I heard my father blaming mother instead,
for letting his innocent child and snow collide.

Why? I wondered. Snow came every winter
and he still carried that rage like a sword ready
to slay an enemy his child greeted with joy.
I watched with Mother as he attacked the offending heaps,
flakes falling by the hour, heavy as wet sand,
until the shovel bent in his hands and broke in two.

CUTTING HIS HAIR

When he was five
I set him
on a high stool
like a cherished heirloom
on a mantelpiece.
With special scissors
I picked the curls
from his damp neck
and snipped each strand
scarcely breathing.
His solemn gaze
followed my fingers
as the blades
whispered at his ear.
He learned my face,
remembered the comfort
of heartbeats
and heard the stories
only firstborns hear.

Now sixteen
he lounges on a stool,
the mirror reflecting
torso and fair head
inclined to catch
the sound of surf
and girls passing.
He smiles
his own thoughts
and what I murmur
falls on deaf ears.

Tufts spring
through my fingers
as he yearns
behind closed eyes.
Toweling cuttings
from his shoulder,
I think about

that clever lady long ago
who cropped a hero
as he lay in her lap
dreaming of anywhere
but where he was.

THE REDDISH EGRET

Shaggy as a duster,
rusty from the chest up,
he's quite a sight
prancing into the shallows,
bandy legs spread,
wings out like awnings.
A consummate intimidator,
he storms lagoons in a flurry
of salt and spray,
driving little fishy prey
ahead in panic.
His next of kin, the Little,
the Snowy, the Great,
poise silent in the weeds,
piercing a meal with dagger beaks
before they're even noticed.
The marshes teem with them.

The Reddish doesn't know
he's rare and running early
to an uncertain future.
That drunken reckless stagger
has kept him living on and lively.
A lucky swish and snap
at minnows in a panic
will sometimes snag
another mouthful.

One might say he's not
too bright, his methods born
of a random quirk of evolution.
Flashing feathers seems,
for now, to work for him,
a misbegotten byway
putting off the moment
he'll be striding the inlets
for a farewell appearance.

THE BULLFROGS OF WEYMOUTH

Hour by hour the moon climbs the weeping cherry
and fat inflating throats

erupt the loud unlovely "jug-o-rum"
into the warm night air.

Tadpoles of the season
plump up in algae luxury

and wigglers teem in the depths
on their way to swarm and liftoff.

By day a heron keeps a vigil
with a Grecian statue

and water lilies, creamy as porcelain,
glow in the corners of the formal pool.

Tossing in unfamiliar beds, we turn to the moon
and stars and moths at the window.

The bullfrogs' music enters us
and invades our waking dreams

with their own version of enticement
but sleep's elusive

as we burrow in our pillows and wonder
how such unlikely love calls

bring reluctant
she-frogs in.

RISOTTO

As I push the spoon around, I'm tipsy in the steam
and wine fumes rising from the pot, misting my glasses
and the kitchen window, the rice softening,
the cheese melting, the commandment "keep stirring"
a welcome lapse in a day full of demands.

I am mindless as a clam fanning its gills
in the bracing wash of a new tide,
my eyes closed, my body bending
and swaying, a readiness for contention
long gone as my spine weakens
in the broth of stove captivity.

When it's done, I'm steeping in placidity,
tinctures of thyme and bay
have knocked me silly. With downcast eyes,
I bring it to the table in a blue clay dish.

After dinner, when the evening comes
to a close, and my hair and hands murmur
"risotto," he leans my way the better to listen.
The candle burns down and we drain
our glasses to the lees. As he leads me away
to our bed in a cloud of herbs and oil,
he thinks it's *his* idea.

GRATITUDE

Three sets of tennis, and my looping forehand
    caught the back corner.
Delicious, the way the heart leaps
    and tumbles. I'm standing
on our shadowy back porch—

I can hear my neighbor,
reading *Little Lamb, who made thee?*
to his daughters. His voice and theirs
make a little sunset music, flutes
and viola da gamba, soon to end
    with the bedtime hour.

A step at the door. The scuff
and jingle I know so well.
    Come outside, my love,
There's a possum in the compost
and the frogs are tuning up.

The neighborhood owl's calling in the oak.
    The screens are building
a collection of moths, and the moment's
down to a trusty body's good ache
    and gratitude.

Sweat cools on my bare arms
    like a blessing.
I'm drinking the first gulps
of cold beer, a burst of yesses
    flooding my mouth.

NAME HUNT ON THE ENO

On a cold day in early spring, the stream swollen
by melted snow and a recent downpour,
three heads search the ground
for any early sprout or bloom
to show itself. And there—a patch
of mottled leaves and tiny yellow-brownish
flowers nods above the mat of last fall's leaves.

Grimacing to be the first to put a label
on the damn intriguing thing, we white-haired
would-be botanists begin the all-too-familiar process:
fishing in our brains for names in hiding.

Edna comes up with "Dogtooth Violet"
and, while we slow-witted strivers frown
and squint, Martha mumbles "Lily, Trout."
I have the feeling there's another name out there,
its ghost an itch I can't quite scratch.

It bloomed in another early spring
when I stood in a woodsy place with a man
who had no trouble finding words to disavow
our love and leave me for another.

As the stream gurgles its old music
and I look down at my sturdy shoes
side by side among the little yellow traitors,
the third and final name sizzles from my memory,
the lowly, lovely "Adder's Tongue."

ASH LIGHT

The new moon,
dusky and mottled,
shows a face
of loss I never noticed
       when I wanted radiance.

Now I gravitate
to the dark,
the suspicious x-ray,
smudges under the eyes
       of a friend,

and spread wings
over roadkill.
Most lights seem
too bright,
       most smiles too wide.

Give me smoke and shade,
and crannies
where far corners
lie beyond
       a torch's reach.

Tonight, in a web of stars,
I see her rising,
the old lady
with her secrets,
       almost invisible.

ASTRONOMER

You were born
zipped up and inscrutable.
Escapee of crib and collar,
Houdini of splints and knots,
stitched and scarred,
you were chest-close
with whereabouts,
and hows and whys.
No songster, you
were one sweet clam.

Forty years
and you've gravitated
to an expansive view.
Your beat is planets,
the far and fugitive.
You grope infinity
in small increments,
and take the measure of
wobbles and nudges.

You're a father now
with a boy of your own,
slow to smile and
tight with his thoughts,
heir to your errant
gene for reticence.
Maybe that's the reason
you call me often now,
making up for time lost,
sharing news
from the Milky Way
and another exo object
for your crown.

MUSIC LESSONS

Sitting with my parents in concert halls,
feeling the brass and strings
stroke my solar plexus,
I discovered in myself
a lasting home: the pleasure
of labor toward something
just out of reach.

Not even Mr. Heinrich's whisper
to my mother, "Madam, you're wasting
your money," dulled my appetite for hours
at our Baldwin, following the metronome
up and down the scales, passionate
for the moments, rare and fleeting,
when hands and heart connected,
and the music's beauty lifted me
beyond my slow-fingered striving.

Now my daughter weeps in my arms,
her work, marriage, life
a weight she can't bear right now.
Cradling her warm thinness, I think
I have never held her enough.
I bask in her nearness, linger
for the tender weight of her
against my chest. In a minute

I'll tell her this: whatever
my wrong moves—impetuous,
risky, self-indulgent—those deeds
were practice, exercises carried out
in a life cluttered and solitary,
where every day, lost to the possibility
of mastery, I stretched for improvement,
picking out rough chords, all night
sometimes, my fingers cramping.

RICE PUDDING

Think of it in blue porcelain,
the bowl one of a kind. *Just for me?*
I asked her, as she spooned

the special cream from its shell-thin
depths, and I raised my head
from my sickbed. "Weak lungs"

gave me whole winters
of bronchitis and pneumonia,
delicious lazy solitudes I wiled away

with radio soaps, piles of books,
and special treats prepared, with
banging of pans by my mother,

who felt guilty, I think, for having
a sickly specimen for a daughter.
Since then, in out-of-the-way tearooms

or small-town cafes, rice pudding
has been stale and the raisins sparse,
but close my eyes—and there's Mama's

cool hand on my forehead, Stella Dallas
on the Philco, and nothing in the world
to do or win or be.

INTERMITTENT

[*The* News and Observer *reports that intermittent waterways, streams that dry up in the summer, will no longer get federal protection under new administration proposals.*]

It's shining now, an imperfect oval
reflecting gray sky, and the bare branches
of this winter landscape, its glitter
visible from our bedroom window
where I stand testing my sore knee,
arthritic and on its way to seizing up.
After a parched autumn, leaves turning brown,
path to the easement rubbly with twigs and grit,
torrents of December rain sent this tiny pool
to us, filling a natural dip, widening
from a puddle to its present
                twelve-foot grandeur.

My eyes take in the brush piles stacked
with branches from an ice storm,
the compost heap scattered
by midnight raccoons and the feeders
already bouncing with early chickadees.
A matchstick deer takes shape
against the pond's mirror, browsing winter-sere grasses
at the water's edge. She swings her nose up,
flicks an ear and twists
                away into the briars.

Yesterday, a hawk sat on the power pole
across the pond, its silhouette
giving me such a strange pang
I fear the world will never touch me
like this again. Who can tell
when it's the last high note,
                the last hard climb?

I'm fierce now for permanence. Let me have
tadpoles and newts and a spring chorus of frogs,

even a vigorous hatch of mosquitoes in May
if it means water's pooling.
I want to watch blackberries down there
bloom and set fruit,
to gather a bucketful for jam
                    before the waxwings strip the canes.

I want *intermittent* to mean what it says—
a spiraling away, a confident returning—
whether I stand at this window
or sit with a crutch and a blanket over my knees,
or—hawk overhead, woodland greening—
                    I'm dead and gone to compost.

ANYWHERE

I've lived in tents, slept in cars,
on friends' sofas, and strange floors.
They fit me like my favorite blue jeans
compared to our one-size-fits-all-
retirement "village," where cosseting

and care's on offer when it's needed.
Vigor on the wane, on our last slide
to extinction, my husband and I have moved
to a cookie-cutter cottage
and made a home.

Most nights in dreams, I find
the self I used to be, slipping back
into the frayed T-shirts and tennis sweats
of a life that suited us, a view
of the woods and a bedroom where the full moon's
light flooded our pillows and woke us to love.

Everyone here has a window on everyone else:
have a drink at midnight on your front stoop,
swear at your wife at dinner, or break a leg in your tub,
and it's fodder for the grapevine by coffee hour,
gossip that beats back boredom, and stirs
self-recognition—and compassion.

You can live anywhere, my friend says,
and, truth to tell, I've thrived in many spaces.

I'm trying it on, this new life,
like a new coat: too wide one day
and too tight the next. But when I shrug
myself into it now, I notice that *anywhere*
is beginning to soften at the seams.

Today, early morning, there are still two of us
at the breakfast table, titmice at the feeder,
and coffee ready to make. Our eyes meet
as we make our daily check for pain.
For pleasure, we'll linger over the paper
and walk to count the ducklings, newly hatched.

READING AFTER MIDNIGHT

First marriage going wrong, the nights stretched
empty and endless, parched evenings inhaling
my own heat under the coverlet,

listening for the click of the lock signaling
his return. I took other lives to heart—
Karenina, Bovary, Vye—

a body of literature, ever at hand
and heaped on the side of the bed
where he might have lain. For months

I fed the hours with their stories,
violent and rich in obsession. They came
to satisfy. At dawn, I gave in to dreams,

journeys begun at the bookmark's door.
Twenty years later, I have another partner,
seasoned and faithful. At midnight, when lust

flicks its lash, before he rolls to pull me close,
he plucks my glasses off my nose,
and smiles until I douse the light.

BIRTHDAY AT SEVENTY

It's almost midnight, and, while the drinks flow,
the party heats up. In every room, loud arguments
deplore the price of oil, the credit crisis,
the losing hockey team.

The screen door is open. Outside the night is cool,
and the grass newly cut and slightly damp.

Out on the lawn there's a giant puffball,
                    white and gleaming
                    as a full moon.
I walk up to it and kneel down to take a look.
It seems to get bigger as I watch—it must be a foot across—
It gives off a yeasty smell. I can't take my eyes off it.

In the soft air, I think of a spore, a being
from outer space, fallen here, taking root,
                    drawing sustenance
                    and fecundity
from the mat of humus under the lawn.

I cup my hands around its dry smooth flesh
and a little cloud of forgotten things floods into me,
a groin aching, a fetus moving,
                    a breast suckling a newborn.

I wander back inside, into the hot noisy kitchen
                    brimming with *me*,
                    celebrated at last,
my fingers fragrant with puffball.

The book was designed by Lesley Landis Designs

CWP

Printed in the USA
CPSIA information can be obtained
at www.ICGtesting.com
JSHW082223140824
68134JS00015B/700